Bears

Polar Bears, Black Bears and Grizzly Bears

Written by Deborah Hodge

Illustrated by Pat Stephens

KIDS CAN PRESS

WILDLIFE SERIES

Kids Can Press

For Dave with love and thanks – DH
To Nickie and Mike – PS

I would like to gratefully acknowledge the expert review of my manuscript by
Dr. Stephen Herrero, Professor of Environmental Science, University of Calgary,
Calgary, Alberta, Canada.

I would also like to thank my editor, Valerie Wyatt, for her generous help in guiding me
through the steps of writing a first book.

First U.S. edition 1997
Text © 1996 Deborah Hodge
Illustrations © 1996 Pat Stephens

Kids Can Press acknowledges the financial support of the Ontario Arts Council, the Canada Council for the Arts and the Government of Canada, through the BPIDP, for our publishing activity.

Published in Canada by
Kids Can Press Ltd.
29 Birch Avenue
Toronto, ON M4V 1E2

Published in the U.S. by
Kids Can Press Ltd.
2250 Military Road
Tonawanda, NY 14150

www.kidscanpress.com

Edited by Valerie Wyatt
Designed by Marie Bartholomew
Printed in Hong Kong by Wing King Tong Company Limited

The hardcover edition of this book is smyth sewn casebound.
The paperback edition of this book is limp sewn with a drawn-on cover.

CMC 96 0 9 8 7 6 5 4
CMC PA 96 0 9 8 7 6 5 4 3

Canadian Cataloguing in Publication Data

Hodge, Deborah
    Bears : polar bears, black bears and grizzly bears

(Kids Can Press wildlife series)
Includes index.
ISBN 1-55074-269-8 (bound)
ISBN 1-55074-355-4 (pbk.)

1. Bears — Juvenile literature. 2. Polar bear — Juvenile literature. 3. Black bear — Juvenile literature. 4. Grizzly bear — Juvenile literature.
I. Stephens, Pat. II. Title. III. Series.

QL737.C27H63 1995   j599.74'446   C95-931856-9

Kids Can Press is a Nelvana company

Contents

Bears are wild

Bears are wild animals. They are strong and powerful creatures with big bodies, long claws and sharp teeth. Bears live in wild places.

Bears are mammals. Mammals have fur or hair to keep them warm and lungs to help them breathe. They are warm-blooded. Their body temperature stays about the same, even when the temperature outside changes. Mammals are born live; they don't hatch from eggs.

Mammal babies drink their mother's milk.

Bears in the wild often live for 20 or more years. A scientist can tell how old a bear is by counting the rings in a tooth.

Kinds of bears

There are three kinds of bears in North America:
the grizzly bear, the polar bear and the black bear.
Polar bears and grizzly bears are huge! Male bears
can weigh twice as much as females. The black bear
is the smallest, but it is still bigger than a large dog.

A big grizzly bear weighs 135 to 390 kg (300 to 860 pounds).
A hump of shoulder muscles makes its front legs very strong.

Polar bears have long, strong necks and legs. Heavy males weigh 400 to 600 kg (880 to 1320 pounds).

Black bears can be black or brown or other colors. Many have a brown snout (nose) and a white patch on their chest. Male black bears weigh 60 to 300 kg (130 to 660 pounds).

Where bears live

Every bear has a habitat – a place that provides the food, water, shelter and space it needs to stay alive.

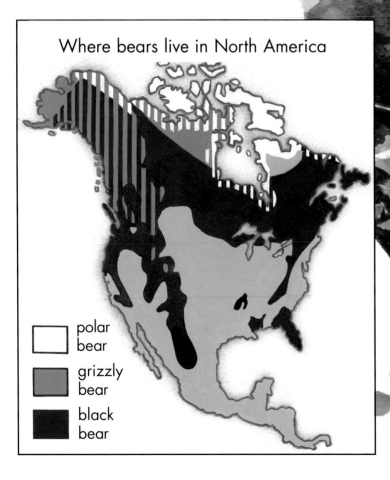

Where bears live in North America

polar bear

grizzly bear

black bear

Black bears like this one live in forests across North America.
They need trees and bushes for food and cover. Polar bears live
in the cold north. They stay close to the ocean to hunt seals.
Grizzly bears live in the west, where there are mountains and
big wild spaces. Grizzlies try to stay far away from people.

Bear food

Bears eat plants and animals. Because they have such big bodies, they must eat most of the time they are awake.

Bears eat different foods at different times of the year. In spring, they eat new green plants and leaves. During berry season, they fill up on ripe berries. When salmon are in the river, bears catch fish.

Black bears climb trees to get honey or fruit. They turn over rocks to find insects.

Grizzlies dig for roots with their long, sharp claws. In spring, they hunt baby deer, moose, elk and caribou.

Polar bears eat seals. The bear waits by a seal's breathing hole. When the seal comes up for air, the bear grabs it in its powerful jaws and jerks it up through the hole.

Bear bodies

Each part of a bear's body has a special job to do.

Snout

Bears use their noses the way people use their eyes – to get information. Large nostrils sniff the air to find food.

Teeth

Bears have 42 teeth. Some teeth are flat for chewing plants. Others are sharp for tearing meat.

Claws

Sharp claws are always out, ready to work.

Body fat

A thick layer of fat under the skin keeps the bear warm over the winter. The fat also serves as food during the bear's long winter sleep.

Fur

Bears have two kinds of fur. Soft underfur keeps the bear warm in winter and cool in summer. Long guard hair protects the bear from insects and dirt. The colour helps the bear blend in with its surroundings.

Muscles and bones

Heavy bones and thick muscles make a bear strong.

How bears move

Bears usually shuffle along on all four feet. Sometimes they stand up to sniff the air and look around. When bears are angry or afraid, they run very fast. All bears can swim.

Polar bears swim fast and far. They pull through the water with strong front feet. Polar bears can swim a long way without resting. They can stay underwater for up to two minutes.

After swimming,
a bear shakes
its fur like a
dog does.

Sharp claws help a black bear scramble
up tall trees.

A grizzly can run as fast as a car on a city
street – up to 50 km/h (30 miles per hour).

Bear homes

For most of the year, bears don't have homes. They have resting places called daybeds.

Black bears rest in trees or on the ground. Grizzlies nap in a grassy place or on a nest of evergreen needles. Polar bears scoop out a pit in the snow to cool off from the hot summer sun. Bears make daybeds close to their food and in a place where they can see what's around.

In winter, grizzlies and black bears live in dens. So do polar bear mothers. Male polar bears usually do not have dens.

A female polar bear digs a snow den. Later she will have her babies there.

A black bear makes a cozy den in a hole among tree roots or under a bush.

A grizzly digs its den into a hillside.

Winter sleep

When the cold weather comes, black bears and grizzlies have a hard time finding food. So they crawl into dens for a long winter sleep.

Bears stay in their dens for up to seven months. During the winter sleep, bears don't eat or get rid of body wastes. Their hearts beat slowly and their bodies cool down. This is sometimes called hibernating. But bears aren't true hibernators, because they don't fall into a deep sleep. They might wake up if their den floods or if the days get warm.

Female bears give birth to baby bears in their winter dens.
Baby bears are called cubs.

109533

How bears are born

Baby bears are born in the winter den. A mother bear can have up to five cubs at one time, but usually two or three are born. The new cubs are tiny – about the size of newborn kittens. They crawl to their mother's nipples and feed on her milk. Her body keeps them warm until their own fur begins to grow.

New cubs are almost helpless. They can't see, hear, smell or walk.

Baby bears
have blue eyes.

How bears grow and learn

By spring, the cubs are much bigger – about the size of puppies. They are furry and full of energy.

Cubs watch their mother and copy what she does. They learn to find food and keep safe. If they don't do what their mother wants, she swats them with her paw. Cubs quickly learn to obey.

The mother will attack if she thinks her cubs are in danger. Black bear cubs stay with their mother until they can take care of themselves – for up to 18 months. Polar bear and grizzly cubs often stay longer.

Cubs often stay together for a year or more after leaving their mother. They may share a den for the winter.

Bear cubs like to play.
They chase one another,
wrestle, hide, slide down
snowbanks and toss sticks or roll rocks.

How bears protect themselves

Bears have no real enemies. Strong bodies, big teeth and sharp claws send out a clear warning to other animals. Stay away!

Any bear may attack when surprised, guarding food or taking care of cubs.

An angry bear growls, snaps its teeth or slaps its paw on the ground. Ears go back, and the fur on the back of its neck stands up. The bear may charge or run toward the animal or person that disturbs it.

Bears and people

Most bears try to stay away from people. But people don't always stay away from bears. People build new homes and roads in wild areas. They cut down forests for lumber. Bear habitats are disturbed, so the bears must look for new homes. If there is nowhere else to go, the bears will die.

As wild areas shrink, the number of bears keeps getting smaller.

This collar gives off a radio signal. The signal tells scientists where the bears are living. This information helps scientists learn which areas should be saved for bears.

Bears need big wild spaces to live and be healthy.

Bears around the world

Giant panda
China

Sloth bear
Asia

Bears are related to dogs. This explains why dogs and bears are alike in some ways.

Spectacled bear
South America

Sun bear
Asia

Asiatic black bear
Asia

Bear signs

Grizzly bear   Polar bear   Black bear

Tracks

The footprint on these two pages is the size of a real grizzly bear print. How does your hand size compare?

Scat

Scat is the name for bear droppings, or body waste. Scat shows what a bear was eating. Can you tell what this bear was eating?

Answer: berries

Bear trees

Black bears and grizzlies use trees as rubbing posts. These bear trees sometimes have tooth or claw marks too. Sometimes pieces of fur are left behind.

Words to know

cub: a young bear

daybed: a resting place for a bear

den: a bear's winter home

habitat: the place where an animal naturally lives and grows

hibernate: to spend the winter in a deep sleep. A hibernating animal cannot be wakened.

mammal: a warm-blooded animal with hair covering, whose babies are born live and fed mother's milk

warm-blooded: having a warm body temperature, even when it is cold outside

winter sleep: a long period of sleep during the winter. Like hibernation but not as deep a sleep.

Index